WALKABOUT

Under the Ground

Editor: Ambreen Husain
Design: Volume One

Photographs: Bruce Coleman Ltd.—(A. J. Purcell) 17, (J. Burton) cover, 18, (G. Dore) 20, (J. & D. McClurg) 21; Eye Ubiquitous—26, 27 inset, 28; Chris Fairclough/Franklin Watts—6; Robert Harding—23, 29 inset; NHPA—(G. I. Bernard) 7, (M. Grey) 19; Oxford Scientific Films—(G. I. Bernard) 14, (R. Redfern) 15; Q. A. Photos Ltd.— 24; Survival Anglia—(M. Tibbles) 12, (F. Furlong) 13; ZEFA—16, 22, 25, 27, 29, 30, 31.

Additional photographs: Stephen Oliver

Library of Congress Cataloging-in-Publication Data

Pluckrose, Henry Arthur.
    Under the ground / by Henry Pluckrose.
        p.   cm. — (Walkabout)
    ISBN 0-516-08122-5
    1. Soil ecology—Juvenile literature.
    2. Burrowing animals—Juvenile literature.
    3. Underground areas—Juvenile literature.
    4. Tunnels—Juvenile literature. [1. Underground areas. 2. Soil animals. 3. Tunnels.] I. Title.
    II. Series: Pluckrose, Henry Arthur. Walkabout.
    QH541.5.S6P58   1994
    574.5′26404—dc20   93-45659
                                                              CIP
                                                              AC

1994 Childrens Press® Edition
© 1993 Watts Books, London
All rights reserved. Printed in the United States of America.
Published simultaneously in Canada.
1 2 3 4 5 6 7 8 9 0 R 03 02 01 00 99 98 97 96 95 94

WALKABOUT
Under the Ground

Henry Pluckrose

CHILDRENS PRESS ®

CHICAGO

When you walk
around, do you ever
think of the ground
beneath your feet?

4

The plants you walk on
have roots that push down
into the soil.
The roots carry food and
water to the plant.

Soil is mostly made up of
tiny pieces of broken rock.
Dead plants and animals
decay and mix with the
rock to form soil.
Does all soil look
the same?

Many small
creatures live in
the soil.
Woodlice like to
live in damp soil.

Worms tunnel through the soil and make spaces for air and water.

Farmers and gardeners
use the soil to grow
crops and garden plants.
They make holes in the
soil for seeds.

9

Many of the vegetables we eat grow beneath the ground.

Many animals dig into the
soil to make burrows.
Burrows are safe homes
because enemies find it
difficult to get inside.
Rabbits live underground
in large groups.
Their underground home
is called a warren.

Rabbits usually spend the
day underground and
come out in the evening
to feed.
Every warren has
several entrances.

13

The fox lives in a
hole called a den.

Tree roots make a
strong, safe roof
and long tunnels
lead to the den's
secret entrances.

15

Moles live below ground too.
They burrow through the
soil looking for things to eat.
Sometimes their burrow
reaches ground level.

Molehills are little
heaps of earth
pushed up by moles.

Voles live in burrows
along the banks of rivers.
They feed on the soft
plants that grow in the
wet soil of the riverbank.

Some birds build nests
below the ground.
A pair of kingfishers
have built their nest in
this steep riverbank.
They catch the fish
that live in the river.

19

Some streams run underground before they appear at ground level. Rainwater soaks down into underground rocks. Over many years, the water wears away some of the rock, making passages and caves.

Some people like to explore
caves and underground passages.
They wear special clothes
and carry big flashlights
when they explore.

Some people work
underground . . .
like these miners
digging for coal.

22

Engineers work underground to cut tunnels through the earth. To make roads for travelers, tunnels are built through mountains . . .

Okslatunnelen

and even through the
earth beneath the sea.

24

In some big cities,
trains run underground.

There are many other things beneath the ground. You can see some of them when workers dig a hole in the street.

There are cables for electricity and telephones, and pipes for gas and water.

We dig into the ground
to make foundations
for buildings.

The ruins of houses, old coins, and broken pots lie buried in the ground. We may find clues to tell us how people lived hundreds of years ago.

Think of all the things that live and grow in the ground beneath our feet.

We use the ground
in many different ways.
We must take care of it.

Index

About this book

Young children acquire information in a casual, almost random fashion. Indeed, they learn just by being alive! The books in this series complement the way young children learn. Through photographs and a simple text the readers are encouraged to comment on the world around them.

To a young child, the world is new and almost everything in it is interesting. But interest alone is not enough. If a child is to grow intellectually this interest has to be directed and extended. This book uses a well-tried and successful method of achieving this goal. By focusing on a particular topic, it invites the reader first to look and then to question. The words and photographs provide a starting point for discussion.

Children enjoy information books just as much as stories and poetry. For those who are not yet able to read print, this book provides pictures that encourage talk and visual discrimination—a vital part of the learning process.

Henry Pluckrose